D1564177

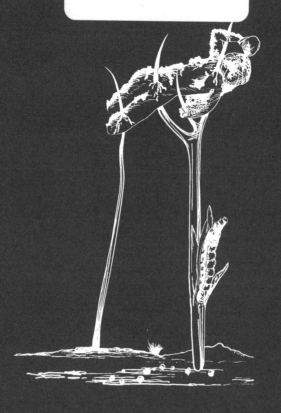

MAY

MAY

KAREL

HYNEK

MÁCHA

translated from the Czech by
Marcela Malek Sulak

drawings by
Jindřich Štyrský

TWISTED SPOON PRESS

PRAGUE • 2020

CONTENTS

Introduction

Karel Hynek Mácha's *May* is one of the most beloved and popular poems in the Czech language. To this day, every student can recite the first stanzas from memory, and new editions of the poem still regularly appear in Czech bookstores. Yet, like many great literary works, *May* was ill-received at the time of its publication in 1836, which like Byron's *English Bards* and Shelley's pamphlet *On Atheism* was paid for by the author. Until Mácha, Czech poets and writers had privileged patriotism over aestheticism. And *May* is by no means a political or patriotic poem.

Macha's rage against a fate that endowed the human heart with a deep capacity for love and passion, but which, at the same time, deprived it of the possibility of satiating its desire, parallels the Czech literary history of his time. The Germanization of the Czech lands after the Hapsburg invasion of 1620 nearly destroyed Czech language and literature. Yet, the international Hapsburg court in Vienna, with its French- and German-influenced Romanticism, encouraged the exploration of folk poetry and historicism and laid the foundations for the Czech National Revival. It also exposed

Czech nationalists to European intellectual and literary currents, which eventually allowed for a modernization of Czech verse.

Historians have pointed out that the tragedy of Czech thought and literature is the fact that it has often spent its strength on the parochial. As necessary as it was to revive the Czech language, explore folk poetry and national myths, and refashion a national identity, these tasks in and of themselves are not sufficient for the creation of great, or even interesting, literature. Mácha's attempt at a great literature involved connecting with European literary currents and universal themes through a passionate exploration of intensely personal obsessions and demons. In the creation of *May* he stretched the Czech language to perform in innovative ways and borrowed from Italian landscape, Byronic themes, and local scandal.

To prepare Czech literature for its new task, Mácha introduced the iamb at a time in which, as Milada Součková, a scholar of Czech Romanticism, puts it, "for the Czechs there was no living tradition of poetics." Czech medieval and folk poetry features consistent numbers of syllables per line, but word stresses per line are not consistent. Czech Renaissance poetry, on the other hand, does feature consistent word stress, with the dactyl the most common meter, since in Czech the stress falls regularly on the first syllable of each word. Another option would have been to use the contrast between short and long vowels, as vowel length is independent of stress. The Romantics and later poets often worked with vowel length, usually in combination with stress.

Obviously, the meter alone does not account for the fact that *May* is one of the most melodious works of literature in the Czech language. Mácha also experimented with various degrees of onomatopoeia, setting the mood of a stanza through the sounds of the words, as when the prisoner's chains thunder. He uses silence, as indicated by the long dash, as well as sound, as when the prisoner marks the passing of time with the sound of a water drop:

> Profound silence — from wet walls
> drop flows after water drop.
> The hollow voices of their fall
> spread throughout the distant cell,
> measuring the length of night,
> sound — die — sound and die —
> sound — die — sound and die again.

Mácha's language is most sonorous in its description of the landscape of *May*, which seems to be a composite of the exotic and the local, the physical and the psychological:

It was late evening — first of May —
was evening May — the time for love.
The turtledove invited love
to where the pine grove's fragrance lay.
The silent moss murmured of love,
the flowering tree belied love's woe.
The nightingale sang rose-filled love,
the rose exhaled a sweet complaint.

Mácha's short life was more similar in intensity and duration to that of Keats or Shelley than to any of his Czech peers, and like Bryron, he was a prodigious wanderer. He loved the countryside of Bohemia, Moravia, and Slovakia, especially the castle ruins, and he frequently visited nearby Karlštejn or Křivoklát, and even once spent an entire night at the ruins of Bezděz to soak up the nocturnal ambience. His exploration of the historic sites and cemeteries of Prague was exhaustive, and he traveled on foot to the Krkonoše Mountains on two occasions. Once he even walked across

Austria to Milan and Venice. Scholars have speculated that Mácha's description of the lake that reflects the white cottages and the prison tower is influenced by impressions the poet gathered in Italy, or descriptions from German-language travel magazines:

> The boats, the shore's white cottages —
> tower — town — white birds —
> ring of hills — dark mountains —
> as if they gazed into a mirror,
> are all immersed in the water's womb.

Whatever his source, though, it is clear that Mácha was an emotional landscape artist. His landscapes are vehicles for his obsession with contrasts, love and death, youth and eternity, day and night:

> But this present time
> of my youth — is, like this poem, like May.
> Like evening May in the womb of the barren cliffs;
> a light smile on the face, a deep grief in the heart.

Mácha's colleagues and later critics considered *May* very

un-Czech. It did not serve or promote a national ideal; it was
not patriotic. Nor were Mácha's personal sartorial choices —
a red-lined cape, a feathered hat — and his Romantic obses-
sion with the individual. Indeed, the poem's tensions, which
stem from a combination of ardent passion, fatalism, self-
irony, and a deep appreciation for nature, seem to recognize
that individual expression will always be checked by the
social mores of the majority. The hero, Vilém, dies because he
has, in fulfilling his fate, violated a social law:

> Whose guilt will be revenged next day?
> Whose fault, the curse I bear?
> It is not my guilt! — In the dream of life
> perhaps I only came to being
> to punish him, his guilt? And if
> I didn't act according to my will,
> why will I die this awful death
> for now and evermore? —

There are certain similarities between Vilém and Mácha,
aside from the singular dress. Like Vilém, Mácha considered
himself an outsider. He was preoccupied with questions of
death and eternity, and he was obsessed with a woman of

questionable honor. He also died young, just before his twenty-sixth birthday, on November 5, 1836. He was buried in Litoměřice on the day he was to have married Lori, the mother of his child. He had moved to the town just thirty-eight days before to study for his law exams at Prague University and was employed as a legal assistant in the law firm of Filip Duras. Although he died in poverty and neglect — his landlord's wife was the only one to concern herself with his illness — and his work was not enthusiastically received, a hundred years later, in March 1939, his remains were exhumed and given a formal state burial in Prague's Slavín Cemetary at Vyšehrad. Although he is most known for *May*, Mácha also published a number of poems, a collection of autobiographical sketches titled *Pictures from My Life*, and a novel, *Gypsies*. His diaries and letters were published posthumously.

In translating, I have tried to capture the exact meter of the original, which means I also depart from iambic tetrameter in the significant sections in which Mácha does. These include, most notably, canto four, and a description of the pre-execution scene in canto two. For the most part, these shifts to dactyl and to a longer meter, such as pentameter and hexameter, reflect a more philosophical or expository tone. Fortunately, even the iambic tetrameter is not slavish, so that the meter never overpowers the language and the internal music of the poem. Mácha made intelligent use of the caesura, omitting an occasional beat in the implied pause of the line. My translation showcases the meter, and Mácha's skillful flexibility within it.

Mácha's painstaking attention to the unity of form and content is obvious also in his language choices. In the Czech, the description of Vilém's mental state in prison, the noises of the prison, and the sweet forest horn from outside, are rendered in words that mimic the sounds they depict. In English there are no equivalents, but I have used words of old Germanic origins to convey the harshness and disharmony of the situation whenever possible, and words of Romance-language origin to convey sweetness and beauty.

I have not attempted to reproduce the rhyme of the poem, though most of the poem is written in an *abba* pattern. The language's seven cases and extremely flexible sentence structure make rhyme sound natural in Czech. Rhyme in Czech poetry today does not clash with contemporary sensibility. Since English sentence structure is not as flexible, and since English does not have as many rhyming word as Czech, the contortions of the English sentence would draw undue attention to the mechanics of the poem at the expense of the highly innovative imagery and the natural music of the original. I have tried to compensate with assonance and consonance whenever possible.

Readers will notice that the style of the dedication is remarkably facile compared to the rest of the poem. It is filled with jingoisms, clichés, and written in a rather galloping meter. Mácha added the dedication in response to the feelings of indignation and anger that the original poem stirred in his colleagues. Members of the Pan-Slavic movement felt betrayed by the fact that *May* made no mention of nationalism, and celebrated such sensationalistic themes as the love between a criminal and his "wilted rose," patricide, and decadence. One gets the impression that Mácha dashed off the dedication in a highly ironic and disgusted mood. Surely adjectives such as "invincible" in reference to the Czech army are sarcastic, given the political reality of the time. The dedication also draws upon the myth of the Czech nation founded on kinship — the idea that all Czechs are "brothers" — which originates in the legend of Queen Libuše and her proletariat husband Přemsyl. I have not attempted to beautify the tired language or meter of Mácha's dedication.

May is a difficult poem. Its images are complex; its sentence structure is unwieldy, and the vocabulary contains words that are unkown to today's Czech speakers. I would never have attempted to translate it without the practical and moral support from my Czech friends and colleagues, whose boundless enthusiasm and generosity sustained me. Petr Kaláb introduced me to *Maj* and to Mácha's romantic countryside, the "lake, forests, mountains and valley" mentioned in the poem. We explored them on a motorcycle instead of on foot. This is the area called Kokořínsko, which includes Máchovo jezero (Lake Mácha), which in Mácha's time had simply been called Velký rybník (the big fish pond). We saw Bezděz, a ruined castle Mácha's imagination transformed to fit the poem. The region is exquisite, with rolling, forested hills and lush, green fields, wild roses, and unexpected vistas. Magdalena Eliášová showed me Mácha's house and the museum dedicated to him in Litoměřice. Markéta and Irena Pavlačíková were enthusiastic and well informed supporters of the project. Most importantly, I thank Michala Kudláčková, Michal Prchlík, and Ludek Bělehrad for entire spring days spent dissecting sentences, looking up obscure words, and delving into complex conceits. Karel Kudláček and Michala Kudláčková graciously extended their home in

České Budějovice whenever I needed it. At the University of Texas at Austin, Craig Cravens provided the invaluable service of reading the penultimate draft for accuracy. Finally, I am grateful for financial assistance from the University of Texas College of Liberal Arts and the Center for Russian and Eastern European Studies for summer grants.

MARCELA SULAK
May 2005

The following poem is intended primarily to celebrate the beauty of nature in May; to facilitate this, the seasonal nature of May is set opposite the different seasons of a human life. For example, in the first canto the quiescent, solemn etc. love found in nature is set against the wild, passionate, unbridled love found in man; and other qualities of May nature are likewise set against similar seasons of human life in the other cantos. The tale this poem relates, its plot, should not be considered what is most important, and only as much of it is given as is unavoidably necessary for the poem to achieve its primary intention. The events take place near the town of Hiršberg, amid the hills upon which sit the castles of Bezděz, Pernštejn, Houska, and in the distance, Roll, pointing East, West, North, and South. — As for any other intentions, as well as sententia moralis, these are more readily intimated from the work as a whole.

K.H. MÁCHA

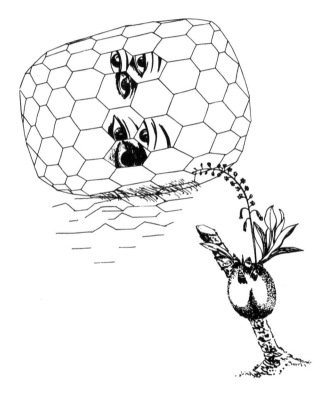

MAY

I would like to speak to the whole world, to
the stars, but — I can only speak to my
nation! and to those few in it who hear me
— and understand me? — No one!!

Mnohováženému pánu a panu Hynkovi
Kommovi usedlému měšťanu pražskému,
vlastenci horlivému, na důkaz uctivosti
obětuje spisovatel.

As proof of his admiration, the author offers
this to the esteemed gentleman,
Mr. Hynek Komm, resident of the
City of Prague, ardent patriot.

Čechové jsou národ dobrý!
Nešťastný, jenž v nouzi lká,
nechť se k Čechovi obrátí,
ten mu rychlou pomoc dá;
byť i Čecha nepřítelem,
nešetří Čech jeho vin.
Čechové jsou národ dobrý,
a Ty Čechů věrný syn!

Věrný syn i bratr náš,
dobré Čechů srdce máš!

Čechové jsou národ statný,
nepřemožen český voj.
Nechť se s vítězstvím rozloučí,
proti němuž český boj.
Čech, kde stojí, krutá bitva
tamť, i mnohý slavný čin.
Čechové jsou národ statný,
a Ty Čechů věrný syn!

Czechs are a good nation!
The unfortunate, who cries in distress,
let him to the Czech petition;
he will quickly give him assistance;
even if he be the Czech's enemy,
the Czech does not grudge him his wrong.
The Czechs are a good nation,
and you, the Czechs' true son!

CHORUS

True son and brother, ours,
you have the Czechs' good heart!

The Czechs are a stalwart nation,
Czech army unvanquished.
Let him bid victory goodbye
against whom a Czech fights.
There where the Czech stands, bitter battle
and many a glorious deed.
The Czechs are a stalwart nation,
and you, the Czechs' true son!

Věrný syn i bratr náš,
statné Čechů srdce máš!

Čechové jsou národ věrný,
věrnost jejich první čest;
vlasti své i svému králi
Čech i v smrti věrný jest.
Bůh můj — král můj — vlasti moje!
poslední je Čecha vzdech.
Čechové jsou národ věrný,
a Ty syn jich — věrný Čech!

SBOR

Věrný Čech i bratr náš,
věrné Čechů srdce máš!

Věrný syn jsi Čechů kmene,
věrný bratr bratřím svým;
jazyk český je i Tobě
otců drahým dědictvím.

True son and brother, ours,
you have the Czechs' stalwart heart!

The Czechs are a faithful nation
fidelity their first honor;
to their country and their king
even unto death the Czech is faithful.
My God — my king — my country!
is a Czech's last sigh.
Czechs are a faithful nation,
and you, their son — true Czech!

CHORUS

True son and brother, ours
you have the Czechs' faithful heart!

Faithful son of the Czech race you are;
loyal brother to your brothers;
the Czech language is to you
the dear patrimony of your fathers.

České hory — české doly —
české luhy — český háj —
šírá vlasť — ta česká země
nejmilejšíť Tobě ráj.

Věrný Čech jsi — vlastenec,
protož vděčný u věnec
květ Ti vije Čecha máj!

Czech mountains — Czech valleys —
Czech meadows — Czech grove —
wide land — the Czech land
most precious, to you paradise.

CHORUS

True son you are — patriot,
grateful because the Czech's May
has woven a wreath of flowers for you.

Dalekáť cesta má!
Marné volání!!

Long is my journey!
Futile cry!!

Byl pozdní večer — první máj —
večerní máj — byl lásky čas.
Hrdliččin zval ku lásce hlas,
kde borový zaváněl háj.
O lásce šeptal tichý mech;
květoucí strom lhal lásky žel,
svou lásku slavík růži pěl,
růžinu jevil vonný vzdech.
Jezero hladké v křovích stinných
zvučelo temně tajný bol,
břeh je objímal kol a kol;
a slunce jasná světů jiných
bloudila blankytnými pásky,
planoucí tam co slzy lásky.
I světy jich v oblohu skvoucí
co ve chrám věčné lásky vzešly;
až se — milostí k sobě vroucí
změnivše se v jiskry hasnoucí —
bloudící co milenci sešly.

I

It was late evening — first of May —
was evening May — the time for love.
The turtledove invited love
to where the pine grove's fragrance lay.
The silent moss murmured of love,
the flowering tree belied love's woe.
The nightingale sang rose-filled love,
the rose exhaled a sweet complaint.
The placid lake in shadowed thicket
resounded darkly secret pain,
embracing it within its shores;
the pristine suns of other worlds
were wandering through the sky's blue band,
as fiery as a lover's tears.
The worlds rose in the sky as if
into the shrine of lasting love
till — passion burned itself away,
diminishing to sparks, it died —
wandering, these lovers joined as one.

Ouplné lůny krásná tvář —
tak bledě jasná jasně bledá,
jak milence milenka hledá —
ve růžovou vzplanula zář;
na vodách obrazy své zřela,
a sama k sobě láskou mřela.
Dál blyštil bledý dvorů stín,
jenž k sobě šly vzdy blíž a blíž,
jak v objetí by níž a níž,
se vinuly v soumraku klín,
až posléz šerem v jedno splynou.
S nimi se stromy k stromům vinou. —
Nejzáze stíní šero hor,
tam bříza k boru, k bříze bor
se kloní. Vlna za vlnou
potokem spěchá. Vře plnou —
v čas lásky — láskou každý tvor.

Za růžového večera
pod dubem sličná děva sedí,
se skály v břehu jezera
daleko přes jezero hledí.

The lovely face of the full moon —
so palely light, so lightly pale,
like one, beloved, seeks her love —
enflamed into a rosy flush
because she'd seen her watery face,
and she was dying of love for herself.
The far white cottages' images glowed
and drew together, closer, close,
as if embracing, lower, low,
then flowed into the sunset's womb,
there finally in the twilight merged into one.
With them, the trees converged with trees. —
Behind, the mountains cast their gloom,
where birch to pine and pine to birch
inclined. And wave pursuing wave
rushed through the stream. Yes, every being —
in love's time — overflowed with love.

Beneath an oak this rosy eve
a comely girl is sitting. From
a rock above the shore, across
the lake she gazes.

To se jí modro k nohoum vine,
dále zeleně zakvítá,
vzdy zeleněji prosvítá,
až v dálce v bledé jasno splyne.
Po šírošíré hladině
umdlelý dívka zrak upírá;
po šírošíré hladině
nic mimo promyk hvězd nezírá.
Dívčina krásná, anjel padlý,
co amarant na jaro svadlý,
v ubledlých lících krásy spějí.
Hodina, jenž jí všecko vzala,
ta v usta, zraky, čelo její
půvabný žal i smutek psala. —

Tak zašel dnes dvacátý den,
v krajinu tichou kráčí sen.
Poslední požár kvapně hasne,
i nebe, jenž se růžojasné
nad modrými horami míhá.
"On nejde! — již se nevrátí! —
Svedenou žel tu zachvátí!"
Hluboký vzdech jí ňádra zdvíhá,

Here blue is winding to her legs,
it flowers further into green,
and ever greener, till it flows
and merges into pallid light.
Across the vastness of the lake
her anxious, weary eyes are fixed;
across the vastness of the lake
only stars reflect their light.
Such a lovely, fallen angel,
amaranth of barren spring,
the sleeping beauty of her face.
This hour has stolen everything,
and marked her forehead, eyes and mouth
with sadness and a charming grief. —

Today, the twentieth, subsided
like dreams crossing the countryside.
The final blaze of sunset goes,
and then the sky, grown lately rose,
falters over far blue hills.
"He isn't coming! — He won't return! —"
The girl, betrayed, is torn by grief!
A deep sigh rises on her chest,

bolestný srdcem bije cit,
a u tajemné vod stonání
mísí se dívky pláč a lkání.
V slzích se zhlíží hvězdný svit,
jenž po lících co jiskry plynou.
Vřelé ty jiskry tváře chladné
co padající hvězdy hynou;
kam zapadnou, tam květ uvadne.

Viz, mihla se u skály kraje;
daleko přes ní nahnuté
větýrek bílým šatem vlaje.
Oko má v dálku napnuté. —
Teď slzy rychle utírá,
rukou si zraky zastírá
upírajíc je v dálné kraje,
kde jezero se v hory kloní,
po vlnách jiskra jiskru honí,
po vodě hvězda s hvězdou hraje.

Jak holoubátko sněhobílé
pod černým mračnem přelétá,
lílie vodní zakvétá

her heart is throbbing painfully,
and in the waters strange, soft moans
are mixing with her tears and grief.
The starlight preens itself in tears
that flow across her cheeks like sparks;
the sparks are hot, her cheeks are cold.
They die, like falling stars,
and where they fall, the flowers fold.

And see, she flickers at the edge
and leans across the rock, the breeze
is blowing through her soft white dress;
into the distance her eyes gaze. —
But now she quickly dries her tears
and shades her eyes with her pale hand
to gaze across the distant land
to where the lake slides into hills.
The sparkles chase across the waves,
star plays with star across the lake.

Now like a snow-white dove
that flies beneath black clouds, or like
a water lily in full bloom,

nad temné modro, tak se číle —
kde jezero se v hory níží —
po temných vlnách cosi blíží,
rychle se blíží. Malá chvíle,
a již co čápa vážný let,
ne již holoubě či lílie květ,
bílá se plachta větrem houpá.
Štíhlé se veslo v modru koupá,
a dlouhé pruhy kolem tvoří.
Těm zlaté růže, jenž při doubí
tam na horách po nebi hoří,
růžovým zlatem čela broubí.
"Rychlý to člůnek! blíž a blíže!
To on, to on! Ty péra, kvítí,
klobouk, oko, jenž pod ním svítí,
ten plášť!" Již člůn pod skalou víže.

Vzhůru po skále lehký krok
uzounkou stezkou plavce vede.
Dívce se zardí tváře bledé;
za dub je skryta. — Vstříc mu běží,
zaplesá — běží — dlouhý skok —
již plavci, již na prsou leží —

so quick above the darkened blue —
where the lake slopes to the hills —
it comes upon the dark waves' frills,
it comes so quick. A moment, two,
now like a stork in solemn flight,
no longer like a dove or lily,
this white sail swings on the wind.
The slender oar, now bathed in blue
releases ripples all about.
Above the hilltops golden roses
that burn in oak groves against the sky
imprint the prow with rosy gold.
"That rapid skiff that's drawing near!
It's him! It's him! Those feathers and flower,
that hat, and under glow his eyes,
that cloak!" He ties the boat beneath the cliff.

He climbs the rock with agile steps,
and up the narrow path he comes.
The girl's pale cheeks are blushing rose.
Behind an oak she hides, — then runs,
rejoicing — running — now a leap
that lands her firm against his chest.

"Ha! Běda mi!" Vtom lůny zář
jí známou osvítila tvář;
hrůzou se krev jí v žilách staví.
"Kde Vilém můj?"

          "Viz," plavec k ní
tichými slovy šepce praví:
"Tam při jezeru vížka ční
nad stromů noc; její bílý stín
hlubokoť stopen v jezera klín;
však hlouběji ještě u vodu vryt
je z mala okénka lampy svit;
tam Vilém myšlenkou se baví,
že příští den jej žití zbaví.
On hanu svou, on tvoji vinu
se dozvěděl; on svůdce tvého
vraždě zavraždil otce svého!
Msta v patách kráčí jeho činu. —
Hanebně zemře. — Poklid mu dán,
až tváře, jenž co růže květou,
zbledlé nad kolem obdrží stán,
až štíhlé oudy v kolo vpletou.

"Ha! Woe is me!" In the moonlight
a face she knows is lit for her.
Her blood runs cold with fear.
"Where is my Vilém?"

        "Look," the boatman says
with words that only she can hear:
"There by the lake, a tower rises
above the night of trees; its white form
is drowning in the lake's dark womb;
see, where the lamplight from that window
engraves itself on the water,
there Vilém entertains himself
with thoughts of how tomorrow frees
him from this life. He's learned his shame,
your guilt; in killing your seducer
he murdered his own father!
Revenge now follows the heels of this act. —
He'll die in shame. — He'll have no peace,
until his face, now like a rose,
whitens on the wheel. He'll take his rest
with slender limbs wound in the wheel.

Tak skoná strašný lesů pán! —
Za hanu jeho, za vinu svou
měj hanu světa, měj kletbu mou!"

Obrátí se. — Utichl hlas —
po skále slezl za krátký čas,
při skále člun svůj najde.
Ten rychle letí, co čápa let,
menší a menší, až co lílie květ
mezi horami po vodě zajde.

Tiché jsou vlny, temný vod klín,
vše lazurným se pláštěm krylo;
nad vodou se bílých skví šatů stín,
a krajina kolem šepce: "Jarmilo!"
v hlubinách vody: "Jarmilo! Jarmilo!!"

Je pozdní večer první máj —
večerní máj — je lásky čas.
Zve k lásky hrám hrdliččin hlas:
"Jarmilo! Jarmilo!! Jarmilo!!!"

And thus the terrible forest lord
will die, for his shame, for your guilt.
May all the shame on earth be yours, I curse you!"

He turns. — His voice falls silent —
down the cliff he quickly climbs,
at the cliff he boards his boat.
That flight, swift like the flight of storks,
smaller and smaller, till, like a lily
on water between the hills he's gone.

The waves are silent, a clear blue veil
drapes the dark womb of the lake;
the image of a drowned white dress shines,
the countryside is whispering: "Jarmila!"
And from the water's depths resounds: "Jarmila! Jarmila!!"

It is late evening first of May —
is evening May — the time for love.
To love's shrine the turtledove invites:
"Jarmila! Jarmila!! Jarmila!!!"

Klesla hvězda s nebes výše,
mrtvá hvězda, siný svit;
padá v neskončené říše,
padá věčně v věčný byt.
Její pláč zní z hrobu všeho,
strašný jekot, hrůzný kvíl.
"Kdy dopadne konce svého?"
Nikdy — nikde — žádný cíl.
Kol bílé věže větry hrají,
při níž si vlnky šepotají.
Na bílé zdě stříbrnou zář
rozlila bledá lůny tvář;
však hluboko u věži je temno pouhé;
neb jasna měsíce světlá moc
uzounkým oknem u sklepení dlouhé
proletši se změní v pološerou noc.
Sloup sloupu kolem rameno si podává
temnotou noční. Zvenku větru vání
přelétá zvražděných vězňů co lkání,

A star has dropped from heaven's height,
a dying star of dark blue light;
it falls through endless realms;
it dwells eternally in falling.
Its cry sounds from the grave of all,
a horrible shriek, a terrible scream.
"When will its falling end?"
Never — nowhere — there is no end.
The winds round the white tower play,
the waves are whispering soft and low.
On the white walls a silver glow
is spilling from the moon's pale face,
although the tower's depths remain pitch black.
The power of the clear moon's light
from window slit through passageway
transforms the night to semi-gloom,
as column shoulders column, circling through
the black night. The blowing wind from outside
sweeps like the sobs of murdered men,

vlasami vězně pohrává.
Ten na kamenný složen stůl
hlavu o ruce opírá;
polou sedě a kleče půl
v hloub myšlenek se zabírá.
Po měsíce tváři jak mračna jdou,
zahalil vězeň v ně duši svou;
myšlenka myšlenkou umírá.

"Hluboká noc! ty rouškou svou
teď přikrýváš dědinu mou,
a ona truchlí pro mě! —
Že truchlí? — pro mě? — pouhý sen!
Ta dávno neví o mně.
Sotvaže zítra jasný den
nad její lesy vstane,
já hanebně jsem odpraven,
a ona — jak v můj první den —
vesele, jasně vzplane."

Umlknul; po sklepení jen,
jenž nad sloupy se zdvíhá,

is playing through the captive's hair.
And at the table made of stone
he rests his head upon his hands,
half sitting, half kneeling,
engrossed in his own thoughts;
across the moon, like clouds they go,
in them the captive veils his soul,
as one thought dies into the next.

"O deep night! You're covering
my village now with your soft veil,
and she is grieving yet for me! —
She grieves? — for me? — only a dream!
She doesn't know about me now,
that as tomorrow's pristine day
begins to lift above her woods,
disgracefully I'm to be killed,
and she — as in my first bright day —
happy, brightly shines."

Now he falls silent; through the cell
that rises on a tower of stone,

dál, dál se hlas rozlíhá;
až — jakby hrůzou přimrazen —
na konci síně dlouhé
usne v temnotě pouhé.

Hluboké ticho té temnosti
zpět vábí časy pominulé,
a vězeň ve snách dny mladosti
zas žije dávno uplynulé.
To vzpomnění mladistvých let
mladistvé sny vábilo zpět;
a vězně oko slzy lilo,
srdce se v citech potopilo; —
marná to touha v zašlý svět.

Kde za jezerem hora horu
v západní stíhá kraje,
tam — zdá se mu — si v temném boru
posledně dnes co dítko hraje.
Od svého otce v svět vyhnán,
v loupežnickém tam roste sboru.
Později vůdcem spolku zván,

his voice resounds, far, far away,
until — as if transfixed with fear —
there where the long hall ends,
it dies in sheer black darkness.

As the silence deep in darkness
recalls the years used up and spent,
the captive lives again his youth,
relives his distant past in dreams.
Remembering his youthful days
stirs up again his youthful dreams,
and tears stream from the captive's eyes.
His heart has sunk in vain desire
for a world that won't return.

Behind the lake the mountains chase
each other to the west,
there — it seems to him — he's playing
in the pine shade his last day as a child.
His father drove him from that world
to grow up in the midst of thieves.
And then, he grew to be their leader,

dovede činy neslychané,
všude jest jméno jeho znané,
každémuť: "Strašný lesů pán!"
Až posléz láska k růži svadlé
nejvejš roznítí pomstu jeho,
a poznav svůdce dívky padlé
zavraždí otce neznaného.
Protož jest u vězení dán;
a kolem má být odpraven
již zítra strašný lesů pán,
jak první z hor vyvstane den.

Teď na kamenný složen stůl
hlavu o ruce opírá,
polou sedě a kleče půl
v hloub myšlenek se zabírá;
po měsíce tváři jak mračna jdou,
zahalil vězeň v ně duši svou,
myšlenka myšlenkou umírá.

"Sok — otec můj! Vrah — jeho syn,
on svůdce dívky mojí! —

unprecedented were his feats;
his name is known to everyone:
"Terrible forest lord!"
Until he loved a wilted rose,
which kindled lust in him for vengeance.
But when he killed the girl's seducer,
it was the father he'd not known.
And that is why he's put in prison,
his body given to the wheel,
tomorrow when the morning greets
the mountains, this terrible forest lord.

Now at the table made of stone
he rests his head upon his hands,
half sitting, half kneeling,
engrossed in his own thoughts;
across the moon, like clouds they go,
in them the captive veils his soul
as one thought dies into the next.

"The rival — my father! The murderer — his son,
he seducer of my love! —

Neznámý mně. — Strašný můj čin
pronesl pomstu dvojí.
Proč rukou jeho vyvržen
stal jsem se hrůzou lesů?
Čí vinu příští pomstí den?
Čí vinou kletbu nesu?
Ne vinou svou! — V života sen
byl jsem já snad jen vyváben,
bych ztrestal jeho vinu?
A jestliže jsem vůlí svou
nejednal tak, proč smrtí zlou
časně i věčně hynu? —
Časně i věčně? — věčně — čas —"
Hrůzou umírá vězně hlas
obražený od temných stěn;
hluboké noci němý stín
daleké kobky zajme klín,
a paměť vězně nový sen.

"Ach — ona, ona! Anjel můj!
Proč klesla dřív, než jsem ji znal?
Proč otec můj? — Proč svůdce tvůj?

Unknown to me. — My awful deed
delivers a double revenge.
Why, being outcast at his hand,
did I become the forest terror?
Whose guilt will be revenged next day?
Whose fault, the curse I bear?
It is not my guilt! — In the dream of life
have I only come into being
to punish him, his guilt? And if
I didn't act according to my will,
why will I die this awful death
for now and evermore? —
Now, for evermore? — forever — now —"
The captive's voice shuts down in fright,
refracted from the darkened walls;
the silent shadow of deep night
invades the depths of the last cell;
the captive dreams another dream.

"Oh — she, oh she! My angel!
Why did she fall before I knew her?
Why my father? — Why your seducer?

Má kletba —" Léč hluboký žal
umoří slova. Kvapně vstal;
nocí řinčí řetězů hřmot,
a z mala okna vězně zrak
zalétá ven za hluky vod. —
Ouplný měsíc přikryl mrak,
než nade temný horní stín
vychází hvězdy v noci klín;
i po jezeru hvězdný svit
co ztracené světlo se míhá.
Zrak vězně tyto jiskry stíhá,
a v srdce bolný vodí cit.
"Jak krásná noc! Jak krásný svět!
Jak světlo — stín se střídá!
Ach — zítra již můj mrtvý hled
nic více neuhlídá!
A jako venku šedý mrak
dál — dál se rozestírá:
tak —" Sklesl vězeň, sklesl zrak,
řetězů řinčí hřmot, a pak
u tichu vše umírá.

My curse." — But deep grief kills his words.
He quickly stands. The thunderous roar
and clash of chains wrenches night,
through window slits the captive's eyes
peer beyond the water's noise. —
A cloud now cloaks the full moon
above the mountain's dusky shadow,
stars rise into the womb of night;
across the lake the shine of stars
glimmers there like long lost light.
The captive's gaze follows the sparks,
that brings an ache into his heart.
"Such a lovely night! Such a lovely world!
How light alternates with shade!
Oh tomorrow my dead eyes
will see these sights no more!
And like the leaden cloud outside
that's spreading wider — wider: so —"
The captive sinks, his eyes sink down,
the thunderous chains rattle and clank,
then silence murders everything.

Již od hor k horám mraku stín —
ohromna ptáka peruť dlouhá —
daleké noci přikryl klín,
a šírou dálkou tma je pouhá.
Slyš! za horami sladký hlas
pronikl nocí temnou,
lesní to trouba v noční čas
uvádí hudbu jemnou.
Vše uspal tento sladký zvuk,
i noční dálka dřímá.
Vězeň zapomněl vlastních muk,
tak hudba ucho jímá.
"Jak milý život sladký hlas
v krajinu noční vdechne;
než zítřejší — ach — mine čas,
tu ucho mé ach nikdy zas
těch zvuků nedoslechne!"
Zpět sklesne vězeň — řetěz hluk
kobkou se rozestírá; — —
hluboké ticho. — V hloubi muk
se opět srdce svírá,
a dálné trouby sladký zvuk

From mountain to mountain a cloud's vast shadow —
A bird's enormous wing — stretched far
across the womb of the vast night,
far-reaching dark so pure, so black.
Listen! Past the hills a sweet voice
penetrates the dark of night,
a forest horn this time of night
ushers in a gentle song.
The sweet sound hushes all to sleep,
even the reach of night lies prone.
The captive forgot his tortured fear
so did the sound enchant his ear.
"How sweet the voice that breathes dear life
into the nightly countryside;
after tomorrow — oh — passing time,
my ears will hear, oh nevermore,
will never hear these sounds again!"
The captive sinks once more — the roar
of chains resounds throughout the cell, — —
Then silence. — And the depths of hell
molest his heart once more.
The sweet sound of the distant horn

co jemný pláč umírá. — — —
"Budoucí čas?! — Zítřejší den?! —
Co přes něj dál, pouhý to sen,
či spaní je bez snění?
Snad spaní je i život ten,
jenž žiji teď; a příští den
jen v jiný sen je změní?
Či po čem tady toužil jsem,
a co neměla šírá zem,
zítřejší den mi zjeví?
Kdo ví? — Ach žádný neví." —

A opět mlčí. Tichá noc
kol kolem vše přikrývá.
Zhasla měsíce světlá moc,
i hvězdný svit, a kol a kol
je pouhé temno, šírý dol
co hrob daleký zívá.
Umlkl vítr, vody hluk,
usnul i líbý trouby zvuk,
a u vězení síni dlouhé
je mrtvé ticho, temno pouhé.

dies like a gentle sob. — — —
"The time to come?! — Tomorrow's day?! —
What lies beyond is just a dream,
or is it slumber without dream?
Perhaps the life that I live now
is just a dream, and the next day
will change into a different one?
Or all that I was yearning for,
and all the wide world didn't have,
tomorrow's day will bring to me?
Who knows? — oh, no one knows! —"

And he is silent then once more.
The still night covers everything.
The moonlight's source removes itself,
the stars do, too, and all around
there's only darkness, the broad vale
yawns deeply as a tomb.
The wind is silenced; water's noise,
the sweet sound of the horn, all sleep.
And in the captive's narrow room
the gloom awaits in deathly still.

"Hluboká noc — temná je noc! —
Temnější mně nastává — — —
Pryč, myšlenko!!" — A citu moc
myšlenku překonává.

Hluboké ticho. — Z mokrých stěn
kapka za kapkou splyne,
a jejich pádu dutý hlas
dalekou kobkou rozložen,
jako by noční měřil čas,
zní — hyne — zní a hyne —
zní — hyne — zní a hyne zas.

"Jak dlouhá noc — jak dlouhá noc —
však delší mně nastává. — — —
Pryč, myšlenko!" — A hrůzy moc
myšlenku překonává. —
Hluboké ticho. — Kapky hlas
svym pádem opět měří čas.

"Temnější noc! — — — Zde v noční klín
ba lůny zář, ba hvězdný kmit

"Deep night — dark night! —
A darker night yet comes for me! — — —
Perish the thought!!" — The strength of feeling
fells his thought.

Profound silence — from wet walls
drop flows after water drop.
The hollow voices of their fall
spread throughout the distant cell,
measuring the length of night,
sound — die — sound and die —
sound — die — sound and die again.

"How long the night — how long the night —
A longer night yet comes for me! — — —
Perish the thought!" — The strength of terror
fells his thought. —
Profound silence. — A water drop,
falling, measures time once more.

"Darkest night! — — — Here in night's womb
the flick of stars, the glow of moon

se vloudí — — tam — jen pustý stín,
tam žádný — žádný — žádný svit,
pouhá jen tma přebývá.
Tam všecko jedno, žádný díl —
vše bez konce — tam není chvíl,
nemine noc, nevstane den,
tam času neubývá. —
Tam žádný — žádný — žádný cíl —
bez konce dál — bez konce jen
se na mne věčnost dívá.
Tam prázdno pouhé — nade mnou,
a kolem mne i pode mnou
pouhé tam prázdno zívá. —
Bez konce ticho — žádný hlas —
bez konce místo — noc — i čas — — —
to smrtelný je mysle sen,
toť, co se 'nic' nazývá.
A než se příští skončí den,
v to pusté nic jsem uveden. — — —"
Vězeň i hlas omdlívá.

steal in — — but there — just empty shade,
there no more — no more — no more light,
inhabited by darkness.
There all is one, no difference —
and endless — there are no moments,
night won't lessen, day won't break,
time won't decrease. —
Nothing — nothing — nothing ends —
no future end — no end at all
just endlessness staring at me.
An utter void — above me there,
around me and below,
an utter void is yawning there. —
Silence without end — no voice —
and space without end — night — or time — — —
mortality is the mind's dream,
that which we call 'Nothing.'
And before the next day ends,
to empty Nothing I'll be led. — — —"
The captive and his voice fall faint.

A lehounce si vlnky hrají
jezerní dálkou pode věží,
s nimi si vlnky šepotají,
vězně uspávati se zdají,
jenž v hlubokých mrákotách leží.

Strážného vzbudil strašný hřmot,
jejž řetězů činí padání;
se světlem vstoupil. — Lehký chod
nevzbudil vězně z strašných zdání.
Od sloupu k sloupu lampy svit
dlouhou zalétá síní,
vzdy bledší — bledší její kmit,
až vzadu zmizí její moc,
a pustopustá temná noc
ostatní díl zastíní.
Leč nepohnutý vězně zrak —
jak by jej ještě halil mrak —
zdá se, že nic nezírá;
ač strážce lampy rudá zář
ubledlou mu polila tvář,
a tma již prchla čírá.

The ripples play below the tower
softly on the lake's expanse,
they join together, whispering,
and seem to hush him soon to sleep,
the captive lying in a faint.

The awful noise of clanking chains
falling woke the prison guard;
he enters with a light. — The guard's soft step
doesn't wake the captive from his troubled sleep.
From column to column the lamplight
flickers down the long passage;
it flickers pale — grows paler still
till its beams vanish at the end;
the empty darkness of the night
shadows what is left.
But the captive's eyes are still —
as if a cloud had veiled them yet —
it seems he does not see at all,
although the guard's lamp spills red glow
across his paling face; the dark,
in its purest form, has fled.

On na kamenný složen stůl
hlavu o ruce opírá,
polou sedě a kleče půl
znovu v mdlobách umírá;
a jeví hlasu šepot mdlý,
že trapnýť jeho sen i zlý.

"Duch můj — duch můj — a duše má!"
Tak slova mu jednotlivá
ze sevřených úst plynou.
Než však dostihne ucho hlas,
tu slova strašná ničím zas —
jakž byla vyšla — hynou.

Přistoupí strážce, a lampy zář
před samou vězně vstoupí tvář.
Obličej vězně — strašný zjev —
oko spočívá nehnuté
jak v neskončenost napnuté,
po tváři slzy — pot a krev;
v ústech spí šepot — tichý zpěv.

At the table made of stone
he rests his head upon his hands
half sitting, half kneeling.
He's dying in a faint again;
the weary whisper of his voice
reveals the torture of bad dreams.

"My spirit — my spirit — and my soul!"
that's how his words, each one distinct,
escape from his clenched lips.
Before the voice reaches the ear
these awful words are once more nothing —
they die — as they were born.

The guard steps up, the lamplight's glow
falls onto the captive's face.
The captive's face — an awful sight —
his motionless eyes are fixed
as if into eternity,
and on his face, tears — sweat and blood;
the whispering in his mouth now sleeps — silent song.

Tu k ústům vězně ucho své
přiklonil strážce bázlivé;
a jak by lehký větřík vál,
vězeň svou pověst šepce dál.
A strážný vzdy se níž a níž
ku vězni kloní — blíž a blíž,
až ucho s ústy vězně spojí.
Ten šepce tíše — tíš a tíš,
až zmlkne — jak by pevně spal.

Leč strážný nepohnutě stojí,
po tváři se mu slzy rojí,
ve srdci jeho strašný žal. —
Dlouho tak stojí přimrazen,
až sebrav sílu kvapně vstal
a rychlým krokem spěchá ven.
On sice — dokud ještě žil —
co slyšel, nikdy nezjevil,
než navzdy bledé jeho líce
neusmály se nikdy více.

Now the guard inclines his ear
shyly to the captive's lips;
as if a light breeze gently blew,
the prisoner whispers out his tale.
The guard keeps leaning lower, low,
bending to him — nearer, near,
until the captive's mouth is at his ear.
He whispers quietly — quieter still
until he's silent — as if he were asleep.

But the guard stands motionless;
tears gather on his stricken face,
his heart fills with an awful grief. —
Remaining there, as if transfixed,
collecting strength, he rises quick
and with a swift step hurries out.
As long as he lived he never told —
what he'd heard to anyone,
and no one ever saw a smile
on his pale face again.

Za strážným opět temný stín
zahalil dlouhé síně klín;
hlubokou nocí kapky hlas
svým pádem opět měřil čas.

A vězeň na kamenný stůl
složený — klečí — sedí půl.
Obličej jeho — strašný zjev —
oko spočívá nehnuté,
jak v neskončenost napnuté,
po tváři slzy — pot — a krev.

A ustavičně kapky hlas
svým pádem dále měří čas.
A kapky — vod i větrů zpěv
vězňovi blízký hlásá skon,
jenž myšlenkami omdlívá. —
Z dálky se sova ozývá,
a nad ním půlnoc bije zvon.

Behind the guard once more the dark
covers up the corridor;
deep in the night a droplet's voice
measures time with its fall once more.

At the table made of stone, the captive,
half sitting — half kneeling.
His face — an awful sight —
his motionless eyes are fixed
as if into eternity,
and on his face, tears — sweat — and blood.

And constantly the droplet's voice
continues measuring time with its fall.
And drops — the songs of waters, winds,
announce the captive's imminent demise —
he lies fainted from his thoughts.
In the distance an owl cries,
and over him, the midnight bells.

INTERMEZZO I

Půlnoc

(KRAJINA)

V rozlehlých rovinách spí bledé lůny svit,
kolem hor temno je, v jezeru hvězdný kmit,
nad jezerem pahorek stojí.
Na něm se sloup, s tím kolo zdvíhá,
nad tím se bílá lebka míhá,
kol kola duchů dav se rojí;
hrůzných to postav sbor se stíhá.

SBOR DUCHŮ

"V půlnočních ticho je dobách;
světýlka bloudí po hrobách,
a jejich modrá mrtvá zář ·
svítí v dnes pohřbeného tvář,
jenž na stráži — co druzí spí —
o vlastní křížek opřený
poslední z pohřbených zde dlí.

INTERMEZZO I

Midnight

(COUNTRYSIDE)

Across the vastness of the plains the pallid moonlight sleeps.
About the mountains, darkness, and starlight on the lake;
above the lake rises a hill,
on it, a pillar and a wheel
on which a bleached skull gleams;
around the wheel the spirits swarm,
a chorus of horror chasing about.

CHORUS OF GHOSTS

"Midnight is the time of silence
will-o'-the-wisps wander among the graves
and their dead blue glow is shining
on today's new buried face.
He, the most recently buried
stands his guard — while others sleep —
leaning on his own cross.

V zenitu stojí šedý mrak
a na něm měsíc složený
v ztrhaný mrtvý strážce zrak,
i v pootevřené huby
přeskřípené svítí zuby."

JEDEN HLAS

"Teď pravý čas! — připravte stán —
neb zítra strašný lesů pán
mezi nás bude uveden."

SBOR DUCHŮ
(sundavaje lebku)

"Z mrtvého kraje vystup ven,
nabudiž život — přijmi hlas,
buď mezi námi — vítej nám.
Dlouho jsi tady bydlil sám,
jiný tvé místo zajme zas."

LEBKA
(mezi nimi kolem se točíc)

"Jaké to oudů toužení,

At its zenith stands a gray cloud,
and the moon reposes on it,
in the broken guard's dead eyes,
in the slightly gaping mouth
and over its clenched teeth, it shines."

SOLO

"The time is now! — Prepare his rest —
Tomorrow the terrible forest lord
will be led among us here."

CHORUS OF GHOSTS
(removing the skull)

"Come out from the land of death,
awake to life — receive a voice,
be among us — you are welcome.
You have lived here long alone,
now another takes your place."

THE SKULL
(whirling among them)

"How these limbs of mine are longing

chtí opět býti jedno jen.
Jaké to strašné hemžení,
můj nový sen. — Můj nový sen! —"

JEDEN HLAS

"Připraven jestiť jeho stán.
Až zítra půlnoc nastane,
vichr nás opět přivane.
Pak mu buď slavný pohřeb dán."

SBOR DUCHŮ

"Připraven jestiť jeho stán.
Až zítra půlnoc nastane,
vichr nás opět přivane.
Pak mu buď slavný pohřeb dán."

JEDEN HLAS

"Rozlehlým polem leť můj hlas;
pohřeb v půlnoční bude čas!
Co k pohřbu dá, každý mi zjev!"

to be joined and whole once more.
What a strange and awful teeming,
my new dream. — My new dream! —"

"Prepare at once his place of rest.
Tomorrow, soon as midnight comes
a wind will blow us back again.
Then he'll have his funeral fest."

CHORUS OF GHOSTS

"Prepare at once his place of rest.
Tomorrow, soon as midnight comes
a wind will blow us back again.
Then he'll have his funeral fest."

SOLO

"Fly, my voice, throughout vast fields;
at midnight tomorrow the funeral!
Tell me what each one will bring!"

ČEKAN S KOLEM

"Mrtvému rakví budu já."

ŽÁBY Z BAŽINY

"My odbudem pohřební zpěv."

VICHR PO JEZERU

"Pohřební hudbu vichr má."

MĚSÍC V ZENITU

"Já bílý příkrov k tomu dám."

MLHA PO HORÁCH

"Já truchloroušky obstarám."

NOC

"Já černá roucha doručím."

HORY V KOLO KRAJINY

"Roucha i roušky dejte nám."

PILLAR WITH WHEEL

"I will be the dead man's coffin."

FROGS IN THE MARSH

"We will sing the funeral song."

GALE OVER THE LAKE

"Funeral music from the gale!"

THE MOON AT ZENITH

"I'll contribute the white shroud."

MOUNTAIN FOG

"I'll provide the mourning veils."

NIGHT

"I'll distribute the black vestures."

MOUNTAINS IN SURROUNDING COUNTRYSIDE

"Give us vestures, give us veils."

PADAJÍCÍ ROSA

"A já vám slzy zapůjčím."

SUCHOPAR

"Pak já rozduji vonný dým."

ZAPADAJÍCÍ MRAČNO

"Já rakev deštěm pokropím."

PADAJÍCÍ KVĚT

"Já k tomu věnce uviji."

LEHKÉ VĚTRY

"My na rakev je donesem."

SVATOJÁNSKÉ MUŠKY

"My drobné svíce ponesem."

BOUŘE Z HLUBOKA

"Já zvonů dutý vzbudím hlas."

FALLING DEW

"And I will lend you tears."

WASTELAND

"Then I will breathe a pleasant fragrance."

SETTING CLOUD

"I'll sprinkle on the coffin rain."

FALLING FLOWER

"I will make the wreaths for it."

LIGHT WINDS

"We will take them to the coffin."

FIREFLIES

"Little candles we will bring."

STORM FROM THE DEEP

"I will awake the hollow bells."

KRTEK POD ZEMÍ .

"Já zatím hrob mu vyryji."

ČAS

"Náhrobkem já ho přikryji."

PŘES MĚSÍC LETÍCÍ HEJNO NOČNÍHO PTACTVA

"My na pohřební přijdem kvas."

JEDEN HLAS

"Slavný mu pohřeb připraven.
Ubledlý měsíc umírá,
Jitřena brány otvírá,
již je den! již je den!"

SBOR DUCHŮ

"Již je den; již je den!"

(Zmizí.)

MOLE UNDER THE EARTH

"Meanwhile, I will dig his grave."

TIME

"I'll cover him with a stone."

FLOCK OF NIGHTBIRDS FLYING ACROSS THE MOON

"We'll come to the funeral feast."

SOLO

"We've prepared his funeral fest.
The pallid moon is dying.
The morning star opens its gates,
and now it's day! and now it's day!"

CHORUS OF GHOSTS

"And now it's day! And now it's day!"

(They vanish)

III

Nad temné hory růžný den
vyvstav májový budí dol,
nad lesy ještě kol a kol —
lehká co mlha — bloudí sen.
Modravé páry z lesů temných
v růžové nebe vstoupají,
i nad jezerem barev jemných
modré se mlhy houpají;
a v břehu jeho — v stínu hory —
i šírým dolem — dál a dál —
za lesy — všude bílé dvory
se skvějí; až — co mocný král,
ohromný jako noci stín
v růžový strmě nebes klín —
nejzáz vrchů nejvyšší stál.

Ledvaže však nad modré temno hor
brunátné slunce rudě zasvitnulo,
tu náhle ze sna všecko procitnulo,

III

Above dark mountains rosy day
appears and wakes the valley to May,
above the forest, circling —
light as a mist — wanders a dream.
From the dark woods bluish steam
is rising in the rosy sky,
and above the soft-hued lake
azure mists are swaying;
and white farm cottages — on the shore
— in mountain's shade — in the valley —
farther, far — behind the forests —
are shining; until — like a mighty king,
vast as the shadow of night,
the most distant and highest hill
towers over the flushed womb of sky.

No sooner had the crimson sun emerged
and lit the sky above the blue dark mountains
did everything awaken from its dream

a vesel plesá vešken živý tvor.
V jezeru zeleném bílý je ptáků sbor,
a lehkých člunků běh i rychlé veslování
modravé stíny vln v rudé pruhy rozhání.
Na břehu jezera borový šumí háj,
z něj drozdů slavný žalm i jiných ptáků zpěv
mísí se u hlasy dolem bloudících děv;
veškeren živý tvor mladistvý slaví máj.
A větru ranního — co zpěvu — líbé vání
tam v dolu zeleném roznáší bílý květ,
tam řídí nad lesy divokých husí let,
tam zase po horách mladistvé stromky sklání. —
Leč výjev jediný tu krásu jitra zkalí.
Kde v šíré jezero uzounký ostrov sahá,
z nějž města malého i bílé věže stín
hlubokoť stopený v zelený vody klín,
náramný křik a hřmot mladým se jitrem vzmáhá,
a valný zástup se z bran mala města valí.
Z daleka spěchá lid — vzdy větší zástup ten —
vzdy větší — větší jest — vzdy roste tento pluk;
nesmírné množství již. — Vzdy větší jeho hluk.
Nešťastný zločinec má býti vyveden.

and every living creature did rejoice.
In the emerald lake, white choir of birds,
the light course of quickly rowing boats
dispersed blue shadows from red bands.
A pine grove murmurs at the lake's far shore,
its thrush's psalm and songs of other birds
mingle with the valley's voice of wandering girls;
and every living creature celebrates young May.
The morning wind — like singing — sweetly blows
across the green vale scattering white blossoms,
directs the flight of wild geese over woods,
and bends the young trees over mountain stones. —
Yet one scene spoils the beauty of the dawn.
Where the narrow island reaches into the wide lake,
a small town shadowed by a white tower
and drowned within the green lake's watery womb;
a great roar and a clamor build throughout the early morn,
a large crowd pours through the town's gates.
From a distance people hurry — the multitude increases —
always larger — larger still — the multitude increases —
already a great number — its voice grows deafening.
The unhappy criminal is soon to be led out.

Teď z mala města bran vojenský pluk vychází,
povolným krokem on zločince doprovází,
jenž v středu jeho jde jak jindy ozdoben.
Utichl množství hluk — leč znovu počne zas,
a mnohý v hluku tom vynikne silný hlas:
"To on, to on! Ty péra, kvítí,
klobouk, oko, jenž pod ním svítí!
Ten jeho plášť, to on, to on! To strašnýť lesů pán!"
Tak lidem ode všech voláno bylo strán;
a větší vzdy byl hluk — zbouřených jako vod —
čím blíže zločince zdlouhavý vedl chod.
Kolem něj zástup jde — co nebem černý mrak,
z něho — co blesku svit — v slunci se leskne zbraň.
Volně jde nešťastný — upřený v zemi zrak.
Z městečka zvonku hlas. Množství se modlí zaň.

Na břehu jezera malý pahorek stojí,
na něm se dlouhý kůl, na kůlu kolo zdvíhá.
Blíž strmí kolmý vrch, na vrchu vrchol dvojí,
na vyšším vrcholi bílá se kaple míhá.
U volném průvodu ku kapli přišel sbor;
všickni teď ustoupí — zločinec stojí sám.

Now from the small town's gates a regiment sets out,
escorting the convict with measured step;
and he walks in the middle, clad now as before.
The crowd's great voice falls silent — but it will rise once more,
and among those voices one strong voice is heard:
"It's him! It's him! Those feathers and flower,
that hat, and under glow his eyes!
His cloak! It's him, it's him! The terrible forest lord!"
That's what the people fall to shouting from all sides;
the closer his reluctant steps lead him —
the greater grows the turbulence — the more like rushing water.
The crowd, surrounding him — like a black cloud in the sky,
from which — like lightning — sunshine glances off a weapon.
The unhappy man steps slowly — his eyes fixed on the ground.
From the town a bell's voice chimes. For him many pray.

At the lakeshore stands a hillock,
on it, a tall stake; on the stake a wheel.
Nearby an upright summit towers with its double peak,
and on the higher peak a small white chapel shines.
In free procession to the chapel flows the crowd;
all now step aside — the convict stands alone.

Posledněť vyveden v přírody slavný chrám,
by ještě popatřil do lůna temných hor,
kde druhdy veselý dětinství trávil věk;
by ještě jedenkrát v růžový nebe klín
na horu vyveden, před bílé kaple stín,
nebe i světů všech pánovi svůj vzdal vděk.
Umlknul vešken hluk, nehnutý stojí lid,
a srdce každého zajímá vážný cit.
V soucitu s nešťastným v hlubokém smutku plál,
slzící lidu zrak obrácen v hory výš,
kde nyní zločinec, v přírody patře říš,
před Bohem pokořen v modlitbě tiché stál.

Vyšlého slunce rudá zář
zločince bledou barví tvář,
a slzy s oka stírá,
jenž smutně v dálku zírá.
Hluboko pod ním krásný dol,
temné jej hory broubí kol,
lesů věnec objímá.
Jasné jezero dřímá
u středu květoucího dolu.

Led for the last time to nature's spacious shrine,
to gaze once more upon the mountains' dusky bosom,
where he passed his happy childhood days;
again he's taken on the mountain, to the rosy
sky's bright womb, in the white chapel's shadow
to thank the Lord of Heaven and of all the worlds.
All noise goes silent; now the crowd stands still,
and every heart is filled with heaviness.
In profound sympathy with the unhappy man
the people lift their eyes that burn with tears
to the mountaintop, where, in the realm of nature,
the convict stands before his God in silent prayer.

The ruddy glow of risen sun
lights up the convict's pallid face
and wipes the teardrops from his eyes,
which sadly gaze into the distance.
The lovely valley deep below
is fringed by darkened mountains,
embraced by wreaths of forest.
A pristine lake is drowsing
at the flowering valley's core.

Nejblíž se modro k břehu vine,
dále zeleně zakvítá,
vzdy zeleněji prosvítá,
až posléz v bledé jasno splyne.
Bílé dvory u velkém kolu
sem tam jezera broubí břeh.
V jezeru bílých ptáků sbor,
a malých člůnků rychlý běh,
až kde jezero v temno hor
v modré se dálce níží.
Loďky i bílé v břehu dvory —
věž — město — bílých ptáků rod —
pahorky v kolo — temné hory —
vše stopeno ve lůno vod,
jak v zrcadle se zhlíží.
Tam v modré dálce skály lom
květoucí břeh jezera tíží,
na skále rozlehlý je strom —
stary to dub — tam — onen čas,
kde k lásce zval hrdliččin hlas,
nikdy se nepřiblíží. —
Nejblíže pahorek se zdvíhá,

Here blue is winding to the shore,
it flowers further into green,
and ever greener, till it flows
and merges into pallid light.
A ring of small white cottages
hem the lake's shore here and there.
The choir of white birds on the lake,
the courses of the quick, small boats
all sink into the mountain gloom,
sink further into distant blue.
The boats, the shore's white cottages —
tower — town — white birds —
ring of hills — dark mountains —
as if they gazed into a mirror,
are all immersed in the water's womb.
A ridge of rock there in blue distance
weighs upon the flowering shore,
and on the rock there is a tree —
so old, that oak — there — that time,
where the turtledove invited love,
it will never come again. —
The nearest hillock rises up,

na něm se kůl a kolo míhá.
Po hoře — na níž stojí — háj
mladistvý hučí — smutný stesk —
nad šírým dolem slunce lesk,
a ranní rosa — jitřní máj.

To vše zločinec ještě jednou zřel,
to vše, jež nyní opustiti měl,
a hluboký srdce mu žel uchvátí;
hluboce vzdechne — slza slzu stíhá —
ještě jednou — posledně — vše probíhá,
pak slzavý v nebe svůj zrak obrátí.
Po modrém blankytu bělavé páry hynou,
lehounký větřík s nimi hraje;
a vysoko — v daleké kraje
bílé obláčky dálným nebem plynou,
a smutný vězeň takto mluví k ním:
"Vy, jenž dalekosáhlým během svým,
co ramenem tajemným zemi objímáte,
vy hvězdy rozplynulé, stíny modra nebe,
vy truchlenci, jenž rozsmutnivše sebe,
v tiché se slzy celí rozplýváte,

on it the stake, the gleaming wheel.
On the mountain — where it stands — a young grove
murmurs — mournful languor —
across the valley, flash of sun
and rosy dew — May dawn.

All this the convict sees once more,
all this, he must forsake,
and profound sorrow fills his heart;
he deeply sighs — tear after tear —
once more — the last time — before it all passes,
he turns then his teary eyes to the heavens.
Creamy vapors vanish in the blue,
as feathery breezes play with them;
and high above — in distant lands
white cloudlets fill the farthest skies,
the gloomy captive speaks to them like this:
"You, who in your distant courses
embrace the earth with secret arms,
you melted stars, blue shades of sky,
you mourners, saddening yourselves,
dissolving into silent tears,

vás já jsem posly volil mezi všemi.
Kudy plynete u dlouhém dálném běhu,
i tam, kde svého naleznete břehu,
tam na své pouti pozdravujte zemi.
Ach zemi krásnou, zemi milovanou,
kolébku mou i hrob můj, matku mou,
vlasť jedinou i v dědictví mi danou,
šírou tu zemi, zemi jedinou! —
A až běh váš onu skálu uhlídá,
kde v břehu jezera — tam dívku uplakanou —"
Umlkl již, slza s slzou se střídá.
Teď z výše hory s vězněm kráčí pluk
širokou stezkou v středu mlada borku,
doleji — dole — již jsou na pahorku —
a znovu ztichl šíra množství hluk.
Přichystán již popravce s mečem stojí,
jedenkrát ještě vězeň zdvihl zrak,
pohledl vůkolím — povzdechl — pak
spustiv jej zas — k blízké se smrti strojí.
Obnažil vězeň krk, obnažil ňádra bílé,
poklekl k zemi, kat odstoupí, strašná chvíle —
pak blyskne meč, kat rychlý stoupne krok,

I choose you now as messengers.
Where, in your distant course, you drift,
and there, wherever you find a shore,
in wandering, greet the land for me.
Oh, lovely earth, beloved earth,
my cradle and my grave, my mother,
my only homeland, my given inheritance,
this vast earth, this one and only! —
And when your path leads to that cliff,
where, on the shore a teary girl —"
He falls silent, tear falls after tear.
Now from the mountaintops, the regiment
and captive move through the young pines and down,
lower — lower — now they've reached the knoll —
the clamor of the multitude again subsides.
The executioner is standing, sword in hand,
once more the captive lifts his eyes
to look around him — sighs — and then
he lowers them — and then prepares for death.
He bares his neck, his pallid chest, he kneels
to earth, the executioner steps back, awful pause —
flash of sword, the executioner lunges,

v kolo tne meč, zločinci blyskne v týle,
upadla hlava — skok i — ještě jeden skok —
i tělo ostatní ku zemi teď se skloní.
Ach v zemi krásnou, zemi milovanou,
v kolébku svou i hrob svůj, matku svou,
v vlasť jedinou i v dědictví mu danou,
v šírou tu zemi, zemi jedinou,
v matku svou, v matku svou, krev syna teče po ní.

Po oudu lámán oud, až celé vězně tělo
u kolo vpleteno nad kůlem v kole pnělo,
i hlava nad kolem svůj obdržela stán;
tak skončil života dny strašný lesů pán;
na mrtvé tváři mu poslední dřímá sen.
Na něj se dívajíc — po celý dlouhý den
nesmírné množství v kol mala pahorku stálo;
teprv až k západu schýlivši slunce běh
veselo v mrtvý zrak sťaté hlavy se smálo,
utichl jezera šírý — večerní břeh.

Nad dálkou temných hor poslední požár plál;
v hluboké ticho to měsíce vzešla zář,

the sword swings in an arc, gleams on the captive's neck,
the head drops — bounces — bounces again —
the rest of the body now bends to the earth.
Oh, to the lovely earth, beloved earth,
to his cradle and his grave, his mother,
to his only homeland, his given inheritance,
to the vast earth, one and only, to his mother,
to his mother, the son's blood flows.

Each limb was broken till the convict's whole body
was woven on the wheel upon the stake,
and on that stake the head found its repose;
so ended the living days of the terrible forest lord;
his final dream lay sleeping on his murdered face.
They looked on it — throughout the whole long day,
the multitude stood ringing the small knoll;
and only when the setting sun had bent its course west,
smiling in the dead eyes of his severed head,
did the lake fall silent — evening shore.

On dark distant mountains the last fire burned,
the glare of moon silently emerged,

stříbřící hlavy té ubledlou mrtvou tvář
i tichý pahorek, jenž v břehu vody stál.
Města jsou vzdálená co bílý v modru mrak,
přes ně v kraj daleký nesl se mrtvý zrak,
v kraj, kde co dítě on — Ó krásný — krásný věk!
Daleko zanesl věk onen časů vztek,
dalekoť jeho sen, umrlý jako stín,
obraz co bílých měst u vody stopen klín,
takť jako zemřelých myšlenka poslední,
tak jako jméno jich, pradávných bojů hluk,
dávná severní zář, vyhaslé světlo s ní,
zbortěné harfy tón, ztrhané strůny zvuk,
zašlého věku děj, umřelé hvězdy svit,
zašlé bludice pouť, mrtvé milenky cit,
zapomenutý hrob, věčnosti skleslý byt,
vyhasla ohně kouř, slitého zvonu hlas,
to jestiť zemřelých krásný dětinský čas.

Je pozdní večer — druhý máj —
večerní máj — je lásky čas,
hrdliččin zve ku lásce hlas:
"Viléme! Viléme!! Viléme!!!"

silvering the head of that dead, pallid face,
the silent knoll at water's edge.
The towns are distant like white clouds in blue skies,
the dead eyes move past them to distant lands,
the lands in which he was a child — Oh, lovely — lovely age!
The rage of time removed that age far from him,
and far away its dream is like a shadow, dead,
far as the image of white cities drowned beneath the lake,
far as the last thoughts of the dead,
their names, the noise of ancient wars,
the faded northern lights, extinguished fire therein,
the tone of a broken harp, the sound of a snapped string,
the deeds of days gone by, the light of a dead star,
the lost path of the will-o'-the-wisp, the passion of a dead lover,
forgotten grave, eternity's sunken home,
the smoke of an extinguished fire, the voice of smelted bells,
this is the lovely childhood of the dead.

It is late evening — second of May —
Is evening May — the time for love,
the turtledove invites to love:
"Vilém! Vilém!! Vilém!!!"

INTERMEZZO II

Stojí hory proti sobě,
z jedné k druhé mrak přepnutý
je, co temný strop klenutý,
jednu k druhé pevně víže.
Ouvalem tím v pozdní době
ticho, temno jako v hrobě.
Za horami, kde pod mrakem
ve vzdálí se rozstupují —
v temné dálce, něco níže
kolmé skály k sobě blíže
než hory se sestupují,
takže siným pod oblakem
skály ouzkou bránu tvoří.
Za tou v dálce pode mrakem
temnorudý požár hoří,
dlouhý pruh v plamenné záři
západní rozvinut stranou,
po jehožto rudé tváři
noční ptactvo kola vedší,

INTERMEZZO II

Mountains stand, facing each other,
from each mountain shifts a cloud,
as vaulting a dark ceiling,
binding each one to the next.
Through the valley this late season
silence, dark as in a grave.
Past the mountains, which from afar
separate beneath the cloud —
in dark distance, somewhat lower,
upright cliffs appear now, closer
than the mountains were,
and they merge beneath the blue cloud
to form a narrow gate.
Far past all that, beneath a cloud
a dark red fire is burning,
its long and blazing tendrils glare,
unfurl themselves across the west.
Wings of nightbirds trace a circle
across the fire's ruddy face

jako by plamennou branou
nyní v dálku zalétalo.
Hasnul požár — bledší — bledší,
až se šírošíré nebe
noční rosou rozplakalo,
rozsmutnivši zem i sebe.

V hlubokém ouvalu klínu,
ve stověkých dubů stínu,
sbor u velkém kole sedí.
Zahalení v pláště bílé,
jsou to druzi noční chvíle.
Každý před se v zemi hledí
beze slova, bez pohnutí,
jak by kvapnou hrůzou jmutí
v sochy byli proměnění.
Večerních co krajin pění
tichý šepot — tiché lkání —
nepohnutým kolem plynul,
tichý šepot bez přestání:
"Vůdce zhynul! — vůdce zhynul!" —

as they fly into the distance,
as if through a flaming gate.
The fire burns low — paler — pale,
until the vast expanse of sky
begins to weep the dew of night,
saddening itself and the earth.

Deep within the valley's womb,
shaded by century-old oaks,
sits a great assembled ring.
Wrapped in cloaks of white,
they are companions of the night.
Each one staring at the ground
without movement, without sound
as if an awful comprehension,
shocked each one to stone.
The song of evening countryside,
silent whisper — silent weeping —
through the motionless ring
silent unceasing whisper:
"Our leader's dead! — our leader's dead!" —

V kotouči jak vítr skučí,
nepohnutým kolem zvučí:
"Vůdce zhynul! — vůdce zhynul!" —

Jako listů šepotání
pode skálou při ozvěně,
znělo kolem bez přestání,
jednozvučně, neproměnně:
"Vůdce zhynul! — vůdce zhynul!" —

Zachvěly se lesy dalné,
ozvaly se nářky valné:
"Pán náš zhynul! — zhynul!! — zhynul!!!"

Like wind howling in a coil,
through the motionless ring it resounds:
"Our leader's dead! — our leader's dead!" —

Like the whispering of leaves
beneath an echoing precipice.
It resounded without ceasing,
in one unchanging tone:
"Our leader's dead! — our leader's dead!" —

In the distance, forests quake,
echoing the sad complaint:
"Our lord is dead! — is dead!! — is dead!!!"

IV

Krásný máj uplynul, pohynul jarní květ,
a léto vzplanulo; — pak letní přešel čas,
podzim i zima též — i jaro vzešlo zas;
až mnohá léta již přenesl časů let.

Byl asi sedmý rok, poslední v roce den;
hluboká na něj noc. — S půlnocí nový rok
právě se počínal. V vůkolí pevný sen,
jen blíže jezera slyšeti koně krok.
Mého to koně krok. — K městu jsem nocí jel;
a přišed k pahorku, na němž byl tichý stán
dávno již obdržel přestrašný lesů pán,
po prvé Viléma bledou jsem lebku zřel.
Půlnoční krajinou, kam oko jen dosáhlo,
po dole, po horách, lesy, jezerem, polem,
co příkrov daleký sněhu se bělmo táhlo,
co příkrov rozstřený — nad lebkou i nad kolem.
V hlubokých mrákotách bledý se měsíc ploužil,
časem zněl sovy pláč, ba větru smutné chvění,

IV

Lovely May subsided, the spring blossoms decayed,
summer blazed — then summer passed,
autumn, winter, too — then spring arose again,
until the flight of time passed over many years.

It was about the seventh year, the last day in that year;
the deep of night within it. — With midnight the new year
had just begun. The countryside held fast in dream,
and at the lake only a horse's step was heard.
Mine, that horse's step. — Passing through the night to town,
I came upon the knoll, the resting place
the terrible forest lord assumed so long ago;
for the first time I saw Vilém's pallid skull.
Through the midnight land, far as the eye could reach,
over valley, mountains, forest, lake and field,
the whiteness of the snow stretched like a far-flung pall
like a spread-out blanket — over wheel and skull.
Through deep haze a pallid moon was creeping,
at times an owl's cry sounded, yes, and wind's sad trembling,

a větrem na kole kostlivce rachocení,
že strach i ňádra má i mého koně oužil.
A tam, kde města stín, v cvál poletěl jsem s koněm,
i po kostlivci jsem hned druhý den se tázal;
stary mi hospodský ku pahorku ukázal,
a — již jsem dříve psal — smutnou dal zprávu o něm.

Pak opět žití běh v šírý mě vedl svět,
mnohý mě bouřný vír v hluboký smutek zchvátil;
leč smutná zpráva ta vzdy vábila mě zpět,
až s mladým jarem jsem ku pahorku se vrátil.
S západem slunce jsem tam na pahorku seděl,
nade mnou kolo — kůl — kostlivec — lebka bledá;
smutným jsem okem v dál krajiny jarní hleděl,
až tam kde po horách mlha plynula šedá.

Byl opět večer — první máj —
večerní máj — byl lásky čas;
hrdliččin zval ku lásce hlas,
kde borový zaváněl háj.
O lásce šeptal tichý mech,
květoucí strom lhal lásky žel,

and the wind on the wheel would rattle the bones,
so that a terror clutched my bosom and my horse's too.
And to the shadow of the town I flew in a gallop;
I asked about the skeleton first thing next day;
the ancient innkeeper pointed out the knoll to me,
and — as I have written it — told me its sad tale.

Then once more the course of life led me through the wide world,
and many stormy tempests brought me woe,
but this piteous story always called me back
till I returned once more with spring to that green knoll.
I was sitting on that hillock with the setting sun,
and over me the wheel — stake — skeleton — pale skull;
with saddened eyes I gazed across spring's distant countryside,
to where gray mist flowed over the mountains.

Once more it's evening — first of May —
is evening May — the time for love.
The turtledove invited love
to where the pine grove's fragrance lay.
The silent moss murmured of love,
the flowering tree belied love's woe.

svou lásku slavík růži pěl,
růžinu jevil vonný vzdech.
Jezero hladké v křovích stinných
zvučelo temně tajný bol,
břeh je objímal kol a kol,
co sestru brat ve hrách dětinných.
A kolem lebky pozdní zář
se vložila co věnec z růží;
kostlivou, bílou barví tvář
i s pod bradu svislou jí kůží.
Vítr si dutou lebkou hrál,
jak by se mrtvý z hloubi smál.
Sem tam polétal dlouhý vlas,
jejž bílé lebce nechal čas,
a rosné kapky zpod se rděly,
jako by lebky zraky duté,
večerní krásou máje hnuté,
se v žaluplných slzách skvěly.

Tak seděl jsem, až vzešlá lůny zář
i mou i lebky té bledší činila tvář,
a — jako příkrovu — bělost její rozsáhlá

The nightingale sang rose-filled love,
the rose exhaled a sweet complaint.
The placid lake in shadowed thicket
resounded darkly secret pain
embraced by all its shores,
like siblings in a childish game.
About the skull the evening glow
arranged itself like wreaths of rose,
stained the white and bony face,
the skin that hung below the chin.
The wind played through the hollow skull,
as if the dead man deeply laughed.
And hither, thither blew a long hair,
all that time left the white skull,
and drops of dew blushed from below,
as if the skull's deep hollow eyes
were moved by the loveliness of May,
for tears of sorrow glittered there.

I sat like that until the risen moonlight
had turned the skull's and my face paler white,
and — like a blanket — its extensive pall

po dole — po lesích — po horách v dál se táhla.
Časem se z daleka žežhulčino volání
ještě v dol rozléhá, časem již sova stůně;
z vůkolních dvorů zní psů výtí i štěkání.
V kol suchoparem je koření líbá vůně,
pahorkem panny jsou slzičky zkvétající.
Tajemné světlo je v jezera dálném lůně;
a mušky svítivé — co hvězdy létající —
kol kola blysknavé u hře si kola vedou.
Časem si některá zasedši v lebku bledou,
v brzku zas odletí co slza padající.

I v smutném zraku mém dvě vřelé slzy stály,
co jiskry v jezeru, po mé si tváři hrály;
neb můj též krásný věk, dětinství mého věk
daleko odnesl divoký času vztek.
Dalekoť jeho sen, umrlý jako stín,
obraz co bílých měst u vody stopen klín,
takť jako zemřelých myšlenka poslední,
tak jako jméno jich, pradávných bojů hluk,
dávná severní zář, vyhaslé světlo s ní,
zbortěné harfy tón, ztrhané strůny zvuk,

stretched itself over valley — forests — distant mountains.
At times a distant cuckoo called; at times
a moaning owl resounded through the valley;
and from surrounding cottages the dogs would bark and howl.
From surrounding wasteland scent of spices spreads,
the Tears of Mary blooming on the knoll.
A mystifying light lies upon the lake's wide womb,
and fireflies — like stars in flight —
flash, ringing the wheel in games of light.
Some occupy the pallid skull,
then, like falling tears, depart.

In my sad eyes two hot tears well,
like sparkles on the lake they play on my face,
because that lovely age, my childhood
was stolen far by time's wild rage.
And far away its dream is like a shadow, dead,
far as the image of white cities drowned beneath the lake,
far as the last thoughts of the dead,
their names, the noise of ancient wars,
the faded northern lights, extinguished fire therein,
the tone of a broken harp, the sound of a snapped string,

zašlého věku děj, umřelé hvězdy svit,
zašlé bludice pouť, mrtvé milenky cit,
zapomenutý hrob, věčnosti sklesłý byt,
vyhasla ohně kouř, slitého zvonu hlas,
mrtvé labutě zpěv, ztracený lidstva ráj,
to dětinský můj věk.
                        Nynější ale čas
jinošství mého — je, co tato báseň, máj.
Večerní jako máj ve lůně pustých skal;
na tváři lehký smích, hluboký v srdci žal.

Vidíš-li poutníka, an dlouhou lučinou
spěchá ku cíli, než červánky pohynou?
Tohoto poutníka již zrak neuzří tvůj,
jak zajde za onou v obzoru skalinou,
nikdy — ach nikdy! To budoucí život můj.
Kdo srdci takému útěchy jaké dá?
Bez konce láska je! — Zklamánať láska má!

Je pozdní večer — první máj —
večerní máj — je lásky čas;
hrdliččin zve ku lásce hlas:
"Hynku! — Viléme!! — Jarmilo!!!"

the deeds of days gone by, the light of a dead star,
the lost path of a will-o'-the-wisp, the passion of a dead lover,
forgotten grave, eternity's sunken home,
the smoke of an extinguished fire, the voice of smelted bells,
the song of a dead swan, humanity's lost paradise,
this is my lovely childhood.
                        But this present time
of my youth — is, like this poem, like May.
Like evening May in the womb of the barren cliffs;
a light smile on the face, a deep grief in the heart.

Do you see that pilgrim, who over the long meadow
hurries to his destiny before the red sky fades?
Your eyes will never see that pilgrim again
once he disappears behind that rock at the horizon,
never — oh never again! That is my life to come.
Who will comfort such a heart?
Love is without end! — My betrayed love!

It is late evening — first of May —
is evening May — the time of love;
The turtledove invites to love:
"Hynek! — Vilém!! — Jarmila!!!"

POZNAMENÁNÍ:

Intermezzo I

"Jenž na stráži — co druzí spí —" atd.

Bylo pozdě na noc, kdy při pohřbu jednoho z svých
přátel přítomen, byl jsem na hřbitově staroměstském.
Hrobník spuštěnou rakev zemí zasypaje: "Dnes již
žádného nepřivezou," pravil, "může státi dnes na
stráži." Na dotazování své obdržel jsem následující
ponaučení.

Jest mezi sprostým lidem pověra, že poslední na jistý
hřbitov pohřbený přes noc na stráži hřbitova toho
státi musí, a to sice každou noc, po celý ten čas, až
opět jiný zde pohřben bývá, který pak na jeho místo
nastoupí. Takže žádný hřbitov nikdy bez strážce není
a že tím způsobem na hřbitově malé osady mrtvý po
kolik třeba let na stráži stojí.

AUTHOR'S NOTE:

Intermezzo I

"Stands his guard — while others sleep — " etc.

Late one night I was present at the burial of one
of my friends, in a cemetery in the Old Town. As
the sexton covered the lowered coffin with earth, he
said: "He's the last one of the day, so he can stand
guard here." Upon asking I received the following
explanation.

Among simple people there is a superstition that the
last to be buried in a cemetery must stand guard over
the graves through the night, that is, every night, the
entire time, until another is buried, who then takes
his place. Thus no cemetery is ever without a guard;
and so it happens that in the graveyards of small
hamlets the dead might have to stand guard for
many years.

Imaginary portrait of K. H. Mácha by Max Švabinský

ABOUT THE AUTHOR

KAREL HYNEK MÁCHA WAS born on November 16, 1810 in an old part of Prague where his father was the foreman at one of the city's mills. At school he learned Latin and German, the two languages approved by the Hapsburg authorities, and later studied law at Prague University. His great model was Byron, with whom he shared a romantic idealism, wandering the Bohemian countryside to visit castle ruins, always making sketches and taking notes to depict the natural beauty surrounding him. He also walked the length of Moravia and Slovakia as well as making a journey to Venice on foot. Influenced by the Czech intellectuals who were trying to revive the language at the beginning of the nineteenth century, Mácha wrote *May* and many of his poems in Czech (though his early writing was in German). He died of pneumonia on November 5, 1836, just shy of his 26th birthday. He was to have been married in Prague to the mother of his son three days later. Buried in a pauper's grave in Litoměřice, his remains were exhumed in March 1939, as Nazi Germany was occupying the country, and given a formal state burial at Prague's Slavín Cemetery on Vyšehrad amongst the great Czech dead. In addition to *May*, Mácha in his short life wrote a number of poems, prose sketches, and a journal in which he explicitly described his sexual encounters with his wife to-be, Lori.

ABOUT THE TRANSLATOR

Marcela Sulak is the author of two collections of poetry, *Of All the Things That Don't Exist, I Love You Best* and *Immigrant*, and her work has appeared widely in literary journals such as *Fence*, *Indiana Review*, *Notre Dame Review*, *Spoon River Review*, *Quarterly West*, and *River Styx*. She is Senior Lecturer in English and director of the Shaindy Rudoff Graduate Program in Creative Writing at Bar-Ilan University in Israel. Her translation of *Bela-Wenda: Poems of Congo-Zaire* by Mutombo Nkulu N'Sengha is forthcoming from Host Publications.

ABOUT THE ARTIST

Jindřich Štyrský (1899 Čermná – 1942 Prague) was a painter, poet, photographer, and collagist. Among his most outstanding work are numerous book covers and illustrations. A founding member of the Surrealist Group of Czechoslovakia, he was one of the first artists to produce a series of illustrations for Lautréamont's *Maldoror*.

MAY

Karel Hynek Mácha

Translated from the Czech original *Máj* (1836)
by Marcela Malek Sulak

Cover image and illustrations
by Jindřich Štyrský from the series *Máj*
Text set in Garamond
Design by TSP Studios

First published in 2005

TWISTED SPOON PRESS
P.O. Box 21 — Preslova 12
150 00 Prague 5, Czech Republic
info@twistedspoon.com
www.twistedspoon.com

Distributed to the trade by

SCB DISTRIBUTORS
www.scbdistributors.com

CENTRAL BOOKS
www.centralbooks.com

Printed and bound in the Czech Republic by
Akcent, Vimperk

THIRD PRINTING 2020